Ruby

WINDOWS OF WORSHIP™

Ruby Durden

Ruby Durden

≈ REAL LIFE REFLECTIONS ≈

Blessings from Above

PAUL S. WILLIAMS, *Editor*

Stories for Spiritual Growth

Standard
PUBLISHING
Bringing The Word to Life™

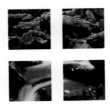

© 2005 CNI Holdings Corp., Windows of Worship is a Trademark of
Christian Network, Inc.

Published by Standard Publishing, Cincinnati, Ohio. A division of Standex
International Corporation. Printed in China.

Edited by: Paul S. Williams
Content editor: Molly Detweiler
Art direction and design: Rule29
Cover design: Rule29 | rule29.com

ISBN 0-7847-1663-3

11 10 09 08 07 06 05   9 8 7 6 5 4 3 2 1

He made it simple . . .

God didn't give us 10,000 different rules to follow. We don't even have to worry about the 613 laws of the Old Testament—set out for a different age. No, as Christians we have just one responsibility. To live like Christ, reflecting him in our lives. I said he made it simple. I did not say it was easy!

So how do we do it? Jesus' answer was simple: Love God with all your heart, soul, and mind, and love your neighbor as yourself.

That is our challenge, to love God with everything we have, and to love our neighbors likewise. My hope is that, as you read these reflections from the lives of people who have answered that challenge, you will be encouraged to do the same. Keep it simple: live a real life, reflecting a very real God.

PAUL S. WILLIAMS
Chairman of the Board of Stewards
The Christian Network, Inc.

Because your Love is better than life, LORD,
  my lips will glorify you.

PSALM 27:4

Presence Versus Presents

We have a little basketball net in our driveway,
about 4 feet tall. Although it's intended for my
3-year-old, my 10- and 12-year-olds like to play
with it too. But they always want some kind of chal-
lenge involved. They want me to pick a spot on the
driveway and let them shoot for a quarter, a dollar,
a back rub, or a chance to get out of their chores
for the day. We have fun, except when the girls win
nothing. Of course, the reason they win nothing

is because they make no baskets. But that seems
irrelevant to them. They want me to give them their
reward whether they've made the basket or not.
And they get mad and storm off when Daddy won't
produce special favors.

Now I know my daughters love me deeply, but when
they stomp away mad, they do their best to hide
that love. And I'll have to admit, in those moments
it crosses Daddy's mind that my children like
Daddy's gifts more than they like Daddy.

Some days I'm disappointed in my children, like
when my girls complain because I won't give them
a prize, even though they've done nothing to earn
one. At those times I'm concerned they mistakenly
value my gifts more than my love.

But that's not most days. On most days when I
come home my girls come running to the back door

to meet me, calling out "Daddy's home! Daddy's home!" My favorite part is when they jump to me, arms about my neck and give me one of those tight bear hugs. I love it. I have nothing to give them except me. But at those moments it is very clear that "me" is what they want.

Wow . . . what a lesson about God and me. So many times I only give kudos to God when he meets a financial or emotional need in my life—when my checkbook is in the black and my stress level is under control. But I am learning through my children that God loves it when I seek his face more than his hand—when I value his presence more than his presents.

I really do enjoy letting my daughters try to earn a dollar or two by shooting baskets in the driveway. But I love it more when they don't win anything and still smile, hug me, and thank me for playing with them. It is then I know that they value me more than my gifts.

God loves giving us blessing after blessing, but he longs for us to be more enthralled with him than we are with his blessings. Isaiah wrote that the mountains should sing and the trees should clap their hands to God. King David added that the rivers and the seas should join in the singing and the clapping. If God loves for his creation to love him, to praise him, how much more is he pleased when his children come running and calling his name?

■■ GREG ALLEN

Do you find yourself only praising God when your life is going the way you want it to? How do you think that makes God feel?

Have you ever felt that someone loved what you gave them or did for them more than they loved you? What can you do today to show God you love him and not just his blessings?

A father to the fatherless . . .
*   is God in his holy dwelling.*
God sets the lonely in families.

PSALM 68:5, 6

All I Ever Wanted

The first five years of my life were great! I had
a wonderful mother who was a stay-at-home
mom, and my dad had a good job at a local
manufacturing plant. Mom taught Sunday school,
and both parents helped out with the teen youth
group. We were a typical Midwestern, middle
class, happy family.

But then, one day, everything changed.

My mother and I returned home from school to find my dad lying in the middle of the kitchen floor, out cold with a bottle of alcohol by his side. The house had been destroyed—I thought we had been robbed.

My mother instructed me to go to my room and get some clothes. I remember saying, "No, what if the robber is still in the house?" She said that we hadn't been robbed, but we needed to get out.

I went up to my bedroom and was elated because nothing there had been damaged. In my excitement, I ran to my parents' room to assure my mom that all was not lost. Unfortunately, she did not share my joy. She was continuing to pack and instructed me to do the same. I was very confused. We should help dad. We should call the police. We should begin to clean up the mess. Something was horribly wrong.

We left for my aunt's house that evening. My world had completely caved in. I spent the rest of my childhood wanting one thing—a happy family.

Maybe you can identify with how I felt as a child—alone, abandoned, disappointed with the people you love most because they've hurt you.

Perhaps you can also relate to the story of Joseph in the Bible. It's pretty clear he experienced despair. His own brothers sold him into slavery. He had to fight intensely for every break that came his way. Whenever things began to look good, he was forced to start over with nothing . . . again. But he did have one source of comfort during those lonely years—God. God didn't forget about him.

God tells us, "I will never leave you nor forsake you" (Joshua 1:5). Joseph held tight to that promise and so do I.

My mom was a Christian woman with an incredible work ethic. Since she worked long hours, I was home alone quite often. I was cared for and I knew I was loved, but I was lonely.

Trusting in Christ, my life has grown beyond anything I had imagined. I now have a good husband and three marvelous children. I live a fairly typical life, complete with amazing joy and occasional disappointment. I haven't forgotten the pain of those early years, but I have moved beyond it. And now, I have a very happy family.

■ LISA JONES

What have you always wanted? What difficult situations have left you longing for something more or for something that you have lost?

What good has come out of these hard times? If you can't see the good yet, write a prayer asking God to bring to mind the good things that might grow out of these trials in your life. Write down any thoughts the Spirit brings to you, and ask God to encourage you with them in the days to come.

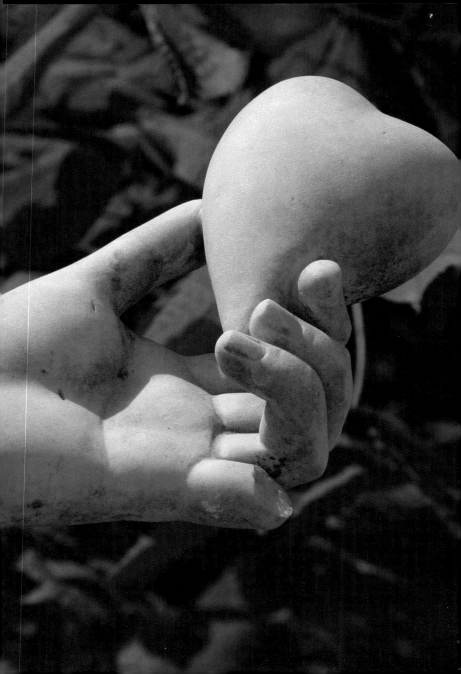

The Lord is close to the brokenhearted

     and saves those who are crushed in spirit.

PSALM 34:18

A Work of Heart

The children at our church were making crafts. The first grade class made little plaster hearts. I was walking down the hallway when one little boy came to show me his handiwork. Just then a little girl walked by and accidentally bumped him. The plaster heart fell to the ground and broke into pieces.

He said to the little girl, "You broke my heart!" and started crying. I felt badly for him. Looking at all the broken parts on the ground, I knew there was nothing I could do to fix it. As I continued down the hallway, I began to feel even worse when I realized that this probably wouldn't be the last time his heart would be broken.

Jesus encountered a woman who was drawing water from a well. She was a Samaritan woman. She had faced the sting of prejudice and racism. Her heart had been broken more than once.

The woman had also been married five times, and five times she heard the door slam as another man walked out on her. She lived in a time when divorce meant she would be left with no possible means of income, no way to support her children. What a disappointment that must have been!

Her heart had also been broken by her own rebellion. She had made choices that left her alone and rejected. Someone said that she was not very popular with the women in town because she had been too popular with the men in town.

Sometimes our own choices put us in places we never thought we would be, doing things we never thought we would do.

Who or what has broken your heart? Maybe it seems shattered beyond repair. Jesus came to help us begin to put the pieces back together. He pointed to the well from which the Samaritan woman was drawing water. He said, "Everyone who drinks this water will be thirsty again, but whoever drinks the water I give him will never thirst. Indeed, the water I give him will become in him a spring of water welling up to eternal life" (John 4:13, 14).

After her encounter with Jesus, the Samaritan woman was forever changed. She learned that life itself is broken, and hearts shattered by it will be shattered again. But immediately she went throughout the town telling everyone the good news—the author of life has come to heal that which is broken.

■■ RICK RUSAW AND ERIC SNYDER

Who or what has broken your heart?
What have you done to try to heal it?

How do you feel when you read that God "is close to the brokenhearted"? What would it mean for your life to have Jesus heal you with living water? Remember that healing is just a prayer away.

[Jesus] humbled himself
and became obedient to death—
even death on a cross!
Therefore God exalted him to the highest place.

PHILIPPIANS 2:8, 9

Louis Braille

No one could possibly have imagined how anything good could come from such a tragic incident.

A 3-year-old boy named Louis had discovered a rather interesting tool and was playing with the shiny, well-polished handle, not paying attention to the sharp point of the awl, a tool designed to puncture leather. He slipped and accidentally put his eye out. But that wasn't the worst of it.

Infection set in and spread to his other eye, stealing his sight altogether. His life would be difficult, dramatically different from what had been imagined. His teen years would find him a deeply dismayed student at the Royal Institute for the Blind in France. He wrote in his diary, "If I cannot discover a way to read and write, I shall kill myself."

And then he met the captain.

Captain Charles Barbier, a French artillery officer in the early 1800s, had struggled to develop a brilliant idea he called night writing, whereby messages could be sent to the front lines and officers could receive the message without having to light a lamp and give away their positions. It was a code of 12 raised dots on paper.

The system was a bit cumbersome and was used only sparingly by the military. Eventually, Barbier

introduced his idea to the blind. Thirteen-year-old
Louis was thrilled at the prospect of being able to
read and write and immediately began to offer sug-
gestions to simplify the code.

For the next two years, Louis worked inexhaustibly
to simplify Barbier's system by cutting the number
of dots in half and assigning them to letters instead
of sounds. Using a sharp stylus, a tool very similar
to the awl that had blinded him as a 3-year-old,
he worked many hours every day punching raised
dots on paper to perfect a new system of communi-
cation.

After two years of hard work, Louis perfected what
became known as the Braille reading system now
used all over the world. He used the very instru-
ment that shut him off from the world to open it
once again—for himself and countless generations
to come.

Not unlike the story of the awl, Jesus used a Roman cross, a ghastly instrument of tragedy, and made it a tool for the greatest triumph. The altar of his supreme sacrifice became our gateway to eternal life, should we choose to follow him through it. The sin and death that enslaved us was heaped upon Jesus. He died a grueling death, borne out of a love for us, that offers each of us freedom and life eternal.

What disabilities or disadvantages in your life, or in the life of someone you know, has God used to bring about greater good? Do you think this good result would have come about without first going through the painful circumstances?

What struggles are you or someone you love facing now? How might God use these situations for a good result in the future?

The wages of sin is death, but the gift of God is eternal life in Christ Jesus our Lord.

ROMANS 6:23

Truth and Consequences

There is an age-old principle that doesn't seem to change. It is that old familiar relationship of cause and effect. There are always consequences set in motion as a result of our actions.

Consequences can be positive and beneficial or negative and even destructive. They can be exhilarating or heartbreaking, public or private, but there will always be consequences.

Even when we're sorrowful and penitent, seeking forgiveness and receiving it fully, consequences still show up to complete what we have set in motion.

This was something that Peter Shelley experienced. Peter stepped into a convenience store, punched the clerk behind the counter, and stole a pack of cigarettes. Less than a week later, Shelley returned to the scene of the crime twice in the same day, but not to rob the store. Rather, he had returned to apologize to the store clerk.

It sounds as if Peter actually could be a fairly nice guy down deep. He obviously has a conscience—his guilt brought him back to the scene of the crime. But Peter's change of heart didn't keep him from the consequences of his previous actions. While Peter was attempting to convey his regret at having stolen the cigarettes, the store clerk was

calling the police. They showed up and arrested
Shelley on charges of strong-armed robbery,
a felony.

Our God is a God of justice. When his law is
broken, there is always a penalty to be paid—a
corresponding consequence.

The way many people choose to react is a bitter
irony to me. They violate God's pattern for their
lives and then hold him responsible for the con-
sequences that follow. That is distressing when we
stop to realize how God has gone to great lengths to
spare us from the most serious of all consequences.

If we received what we deserve, we would have
no relationship with God at all. Our sin separates
us from God and merits spiritual death. But God
allowed his Son to take that penalty on himself. It
has been paid in full through the sacrifice of Jesus.

We have been spared the eternal consequences of our disobedience.

Stuart Briscoe has cleverly written, "Justice is getting what you deserve. Mercy is not getting what you deserve. Grace is getting what you don't deserve."

God took on himself the penalty that had to be paid, and in his grace he offers us what we can't possibly deserve: life itself.

When have you been shown mercy and grace so that you didn't have to face the consequences of your mistake? What did it feel like to be freed from punishment?

How does it feel to know that God has freed you from the ultimate punishment of spiritual death? How can you encourage others with this wonderful knowledge?

*Come to me, all you who are weary and burdened,
and I will give you rest.*

MATTHEW 11:28

The Ghost on the Water

The past few days had been a sleepless roller
coaster for the disciples. Those days began with
Jesus sending his followers out to tell people that
God is doing something big. He told them not to
take any food, money, or supplies of any kind with
them. Jesus warned them: "If any place will not
welcome you or listen to you, shake the dust off
your feet when you leave, as a testimony against
them" (Mark 6:11).

When the disciples returned from their assignment, they were exhausted. They had been so busy that they had forgotten to eat. Jesus said, "Come with me by yourselves to a quiet place and get some rest" (Mark 6:31). That's exactly what they wanted, but that's not what they got.

By the time they arrived at their destination, there were over 5,000 people waiting for Jesus. By late afternoon, the tired disciples still hadn't eaten. Neither had the large crowd.

Jesus said, "You give them something to eat" (Mark 6:37). Now the disciples were starting to get irritated. With an edge to their voices, perhaps, they asked, "That would take eight months of a man's wages! Are we to go and spend that much on bread and give it to them to eat?" (Mark 6:37). Of course, what happened next was one of the greatest miracles ever.

Jesus took five loaves of bread and two fish and fed everyone. But guess who had to clean up after dinner?

It's likely that by evening the disciples could barely stand. Jesus finally let them go. He sent them off in a boat and told them he'd meet them on the other side of the Sea of Galilee. Meanwhile he went up into the hills. From there he could see the boat's progress. Jesus watched a storm overtake the boat. He watched the men, already spent, struggle against the wind and the waves. It wasn't until about 4:00 in the morning that he finally did something about it. He walked to them on the water.

When the disciples saw him, they thought he was a ghost. "Take courage!" he said. "It is I. Don't be afraid" (Mark 6:50). Then he climbed into the boat, and the wind and the waves died down.

The men were beyond exhaustion, beyond frustration, beyond trying to figure things out. In this moment they did something to Jesus they never had done before—the last thing you might have expected.

In that moment of sheer exhaustion, the disciples worshiped Jesus. They thought of the amazing journey they were a part of, and of the extraordinary love of this man Jesus; and reaching deep into their tired souls, they worshiped him. We don't know when they finally did get to rest. But we do know that in that amazing moment their weariness didn't matter. What did matter was that the Messiah had come and they would follow him, trusting that he would give them rest.

■ ERIC SNYDER AND PAUL S. WILLIAMS

What do you do when you are completely exhausted?
If you had been with the disciples during this tiring period, do you think you would have reacted as they did and worshiped Jesus? Why or why not?

Are you weary and looking for rest right now?
Write a prayer asking God for the strength to persevere until he brings you rest. You can always trust him to give you what you need.

How precious to me are your thoughts, O God!
How vast is the sum of them!
Were I to count them,
they would outnumber the grains of sand.

PSALM 139:17, 18

The Sand, the Stars, and Me

I would like to count all the grains of sand in
the entire world. Really, I would. A friend of
mine, Zach, has already started the count by
numbering 1,850 grains of sand per one-eighth
of a teaspoon. That equals 710,400 grains per
cup. So, I'm set. I just need to count the miles
of seashore for the seven continents, which is
doable, and convert those miles into cups and
multiply by 710,400.

But wait, I suppose that is just surface sand. I would need to estimate how deep the beaches are, and how far out into the oceans I need to go. And I can't forget the deserts, thousands of square miles of deserts. How deep and wide do they measure? I'm not so sure my goal is achievable after all. But it's a valuable project. Really, it is!

If you've ever felt alone, felt that no one cared about you, you could count the grains of sand and know how deep and wide God loves you. Psalm 139 says that the thoughts of God number more than the grains of sand in the whole earth! Even one cup of God's thoughts toward us is more than 700,000 thoughts, which is one thought every minute for a year and four months!

In Estes Park, Colorado, you can visit Rocky Mountain National Park where there are hundreds of thousands of square acres of mountains, for-

ests, and rivers. It is a breathtaking and spectacu-
lar place. But the Rocky Mountains are just a tiny
speck on the map of Colorado, and Colorado is just
one of the 50 United States. The United States is
only one-third of the North American continent,
and our continent is just one of seven. And the
seven continents make up only one-third of the
earth's mass, two-thirds being water. And the earth
is a tiny planet in our universe.

The sun is much bigger, at the center of a vast gal-
axy we call the Milky Way, just one among many
galaxies, spinning around its center at 155 miles
per second.

I love statistics and find them to be really impor-
tant sometimes. I like to use them to consider how
huge the universe is—too big to get our telescopes
and imaginations around. And yet, God simply
spoke it all into being. Statistics haven't been

created that can even begin to describe our magnificent God.

Remember: there are 700,000 grains of sand per cup and it would take 200 million years to fly around the Milky Way one time. And yet, in all this vastness, God noticed us personally. Oh, to be noticed by the one who cannot be truly fathomed, to have the creator of the Milky Way think of you more times than there are grains of sand. It's not the statistics that overwhelm me; it is the truth to which they point. God is wild about us—and that is a wild thought!

■■ GREG ALLEN

What are your thoughts as you consider the vastness of our universe? What parts of the world around you remind you especially of God's deep love and abundant blessings?

What are your feelings when you realize that the creator of the entire universe loves you personally? What can you do to remind yourself of this incredible truth every day?

You will know the truth, and the truth will set you free.

JOHN 8:32

Truth That Sets Us Free

Ever since childhood I've been drawn to search out the truth of things.

Christians believe that the truth will set us free. But Christians often fixate on only one kind of truth. This is the truth that God exists, or that the Bible is the Word of God. But in another realm we don't seem nearly as interested in getting at the truth.

For years I served as an adoption caseworker. When I asked families to tell about their backgrounds, they often regaled me with stories about how wonderful their childhood was. They also said they had marvelous marriages—every one of them.

It was only after digging around for a session or two that I began to discover the truth. Their parents had real flaws, and their childhood experience was checkered at best. And their marriages? Same story. Most avoided the divorce courts, but the decibel level around the kitchen table was pretty high every now and again.

With our foundation in Christ's love, one would think Christians would be the first to work through the denials we create to salve our deepest wounds. Unfortunately, my experience indicates that Christians aren't much different from the rest of the population.

In fact, it is often Christians who are the most
reluctant to part with carefully nurtured denials.
It is as if we think only some truths will set us free.

But Jesus didn't say some truth will set you free.
It is the whole truth that sets us free.

If we are going to be a people of the truth, eventu-
ally we must face all truth—even our ugly personal
truths: the truth that our parents weren't perfect,
the truth that we have serious flaws, the truth that
our marriages could use some help.

If we admit those truths, we will arrive at a deeper
understanding. We will come to understand that
it is OK to be ordinary. It is all right to be flawed.
It is permissible to be human. We are all broken—
every last one of us. Our vases are cracked,
the water leaks out, and the flowers inside dry
out and wither.

We need to embrace life's most profound truth. The truth that, flaws and all, we are loved. Far beyond the bounds of decency and propriety, we are outrageously and joyously loved by God himself. That is the ultimate truth; and if we embrace it, we can finally give up our denials and find redemption in even the most troublesome truths.

PAUL S. WILLIAMS

What things about yourself do you try to hide? What makes you afraid to reveal them to others or to God? How do you react when a close friend or loved one reveals a struggle to you?

Put your fears aside for a moment and reflect on what good things might happen if you were honest with a trusted friend about your flaws and weaknesses. How might you be changed? How might your relationship with that person and with God be enriched?

Jesus said, "Whoever drinks the water I give him will never thirst. Indeed, the water I give him will become in him a spring of water welling up to eternal life."

JOHN 4:14

Dead Batteries

It was 1:00 in the morning, and I was outside alone during a bitter cold winter. I got into my car and tried to start the engine. Nothing. The battery was dead. I thought, *Oh, great! What am I going to do now?*

I did manage to get help that night though. We discovered a faulty component that wasn't vital to the operation of my vehicle, but because it created an open circuit, it continually drained my battery. It's amazing how something that seems so insignificant can have such a substantial effect.

Despite living in the most prosperous country on earth and not having to work nearly as hard as our ancestors did, many of us feel as if our batteries are drained. We wonder where we are going and how we are going to make it through each day when we have no energy for life.

Psychologist and philosopher Viktor Frankl was a holocaust survivor. His experience in a concentration camp helped form his view of life. He noticed that those who were able to survive did so even under conditions of extreme suffering. He wrote, "In spite of all the enforced physical and mental primitiveness of the life in a concentration camp, it was possible for spiritual life to deepen. . . . The survivors were able to retreat from their terrible surroundings to a life of inner riches and spiritual freedom."

The reason for their survival was that those people had a sense of meaning in their suffering, which was compelled by their faith and the hope for what awaited them beyond their pain. When this sense of meaning is missing, even under ideal circum-stances, a vacuum is created. And nature abhors a vacuum. This hole gets filled with work, money, pleasure, food, sports—and it is never enough. Frankl refers to this feeling of futility as the "abyss experience."

So it was into the abyss that God the Son descended on our behalf. And within earshot of death itself he cried out, "Come to me, all you who are weary and burdened, and I will give you rest" (Matthew 11:28). Jesus is saying, "Stop pursuing all the things that never can satisfy, the things that ultimately will drain your life of all meaning." Even in the midst of a prison camp, trusting Christ can provide a source of inexhaustible riches.

Looking toward anything other than Christ to be our source is essentially creating a faulty component that breaks the circuit. If we stay focused on Christ and depend on him to meet our every need, we never will be found wanting.

■■ RICK RUSAW AND ERIC SNYDER

What causes you to feel as if your batteries are dead?
Why do you think that is?

What causes you to feel alive and full of energy?
Why do these things bring you such life? Reflect on
the difference between what drains you and what
invigorates you.

I will give you a new heart and put a new spirit in you;
I will remove from you your heart of stone and give you a
heart of flesh.

EZEKIEL 36:26

Masterpieces from Mistakes

I suppose he shall remain forever nameless. The
man made an embarrassing mistake; and if you
could ask him today, some 500 years later, he still
might be thankful nobody knows his name. All we
know is that a talented sculptor purchased a flaw-
less block of marble from the Carrera mines in
central Italy. Such stone did not come cheaply.
You'd better know what you're doing before you
start chipping away at such an enviable cut of

expensive rock. But the sculptor made a serious mistake and bored a hole through the stone and in the opinion of most, ruined it. The great master Leonardo da Vinci was consulted, and he determined the stone was beyond salvage.

But friends of the young Michelangelo de Buonorotti, who was living in Rome, were convinced he could do something with it. Michelangelo made his way to Florence where the stone was kept in the works department of the church of Santa Maria del Fiore. He examined the still-beautiful raw material and came to the conclusion he could carve a figure from it. Even as others argued it couldn't be done, Michelangelo was given permission to proceed.

In a matter of weeks—just weeks—the magnificent statue of the young David, sling in hand, emerged from the marble everyone had thought ruined.

The statue still stands today in Florence, Italy, as majestic and imposing at its height of 17 feet as it was 500 years ago. Michelangelo turned a mistake into a masterpiece. He transformed someone else's ineptitude into a treasured work of art.

But what if the mistake had never been made? What if Michelangelo had never been faced with the challenge of sculpting a figure out of a badly mishandled block of marble? Would the breathtaking statue of David exist today? I think not.

Now here's something for you to consider. You may be profoundly discouraged with your life at this very moment. You may even be thinking that *you* are some kind of mistake.

We all are flawed. Some of those flaws may appear beyond repair. But they are not. Honestly, they can become stepping-stones to greatness.

The author of life can take your mistakes, flaws, and wasted time, and transform them into an eternal masterpiece. However, you must first submit yourself to his unsurpassed skills and wholeheartedly trust him for the changes he will make.

What do you consider to be your worst flaws?
What mistakes have you made that make you feel
like you are beyond repair?

Write a prayer giving each of your struggles to the
Lord, the master artist. Express your longings to be
made whole and new, and know that he will shape
you into the masterpiece you were meant to be.
Just as the statue of David came from a flawed piece
of marble, what might God make of you and your
mistakes?

We have one who speaks to the Father in our defense—Jesus Christ, the Righteous One. He is the atoning sacrifice for our sins, and not only for ours but also for the sins of the whole world.

1 JOHN 2:1, 2

Cleared!

Have you ever been accused of something you didn't do? The old adage says that prisons are filled to the brim with innocent people. Once in a while, new evidence does come to light, and a prisoner is released after many years of false imprisonment because it was proven that he had never committed the crime. It must be a desperate feeling to be declared guilty when you know you're innocent.

One who knew such desperation was Fitz John Porter. He was born in Portsmouth, New Hampshire, on August 31, 1822. He grew up to be a soldier and made Portsmouth proud of her native son—at least for a while. He saw distinguished service in the Civil War and rose to the rank of major general. But it was at the second battle at Manassas, Virginia, in the summer of 1862, that his promising military career took a very bad turn.

The Union army was thoroughly routed for the second time on the Manassas battlefield, and Major General Porter was blamed for it. Porter was a political football being tossed between two ranking generals who hated each other and who had to blame somebody else for their own bad judgment.

Distorted charges of insubordination were leveled against Porter after the battle, and he was court-martialed and found guilty of the charges. He was thrown out of the army, forfeiting his pension, and was dismissed in shame to return home in dishonor.

It wasn't until 1886, during the administration of President Grover Cleveland, that Porter's case was officially reopened. The investigation into new evidence proved him innocent. He was reinstated to his former rank, and his pension was restored in addition to his back pay. Portsmouth could once again be proud of her Major General Porter.

Major General Porter was eventually cleared of all the false charges against him. But can you imagine someone being declared innocent when they were guilty by their own admission? Our sense of fairness enjoys someone being vindicated after being *falsely* accused, but what about someone being acquitted and set free after having been proved *guilty*? *Wait a minute, give me one example,* you might be thinking. OK. I'm talking about you. Actually, I'm describing all of us.

We're all sinful people, guilty of insisting on having our own way and turning our backs on God. But those of us who become his children are declared not guilty even though we're guilty as guilty can be. We are exonerated, acquitted, vindicated, absolved, reprieved, excused, and even exculpated.

Because I believe in Jesus, I've been cleared! I'm far from innocent but I'm not guilty! I'm free!

Have you ever been accused of something you didn't do? How did you react? How did you try to clear your name? Looking back, do you think you reacted in the right way? Why or why not?

Think about standing before God for judgment knowing that you deserve punishment, and then hearing him say that you are forgiven and all your sin is forgotten. How does it make you feel to know that you have been cleared of the guilt of your sin?

Humble yourselves . . . under God's mighty hand, that he may lift you up in due time. Cast all your anxiety on him because he cares for you.

1 PETEr 5:6, 7

Baggage

A while back I was on a trip with my wife, Diane. When we awoke on the morning of our return flight, we threw clothes into whatever bag was convenient, forgetting we were going to different destinations. When we arrived at the airport, we headed in separate directions.

As I was going through the security line with my carry-on, my bag was chosen for a detailed security search. Several people were watching as article after article of clothing was taken from my bag. The only problem was, most of the clothes belonged to my wife Diane, who was going through security in a completely different part of the airport.

Embarrassment doesn't come close to describing what I was feeling. As the security people looked at me with a questioning eye, all I could do was shrug.

Let's suppose we were to unpack the bags of your life—all that stuff you've been carting around in your carry-on. If we were to gather a small crowd and hold up each piece for others to see, it just might be a bit embarrassing. All the poor choices we've made, all the decisions we regret, every troublesome incident plucked out of the bag for everyone to see. What a nightmare it would be to have to let everyone see all our mistakes!

That bag of mistakes contains our brokenness, selfishness, greed, and lust—all the sins that we hope to hide. We also carry disappointments and heartaches, broken dreams and wounds. The truth is that we don't really like to look in that bag because much of what is inside is more than embarrassing—it's downright disheartening.

Wouldn't it be great if we could free ourselves from all the junk hidden deep inside that baggage we lug around? The good news is that God has invited us to do just that. He has offered to remove the burdens, so we can travel light, unafraid of what might be pulled from our bags and brought to the light of day.

Just imagine every embarrassing moment you've ever had, every disappointment, every bitter heart-ache . . . unloaded into the strong arms of God. If you're willing to give them up, God will take them all and leave only a sense of redemption, relief, and rest.

It's your decision. You can travel this life with a heavy bag full of regrets or with a lightened load, a smile on your face, and hope for a brighter day.

■■ RICK RUSAW

What are you carrying in your baggage today—mistakes from your past, disappointments, discontentment, broken dreams, or broken relationships?
Why are you still dragging these things around?

What would happen if you gave your burdens to Christ?
Write a prayer asking Jesus for the courage to let go and trust that he can replace your burdens with redemption, relief, and rest.

[Jesus] said to me, "My grace is sufficient for you, for my power is made perfect in weakness." Therefore I will boast all the more gladly about my weaknesses, so that Christ's power may rest on me.

2 CORINTHIANS 12:9

Thorns

When you catch a person not listening to what you are saying, they might crack a joke like: "Sorry, my mind wandered away. I must have ADD." I can't say that I enjoy that joke very much because I do have attention deficit disorder.

ADD can make it very hard for me to focus. I often have a hard time remembering things—like when to put my mother-in-law's birthday card in the mail. Sometimes I forget I'm supposed to be somewhere—until I have five minutes to get there!

Now, I don't blame my ADD for all my mistakes. But I do have to acknowledge that this disorder is part of me. Thankfully, I've made a few discoveries and adjustments over the years that have helped me deal with ADD. I am able to focus much better now. But I'd be lying if I said that it didn't still disappoint me that I have to fight attention deficit disorder every day. It's frustrating.

When I started college I was going to be a doctor, but I couldn't focus enough to get the grades I needed. So I studied communications and singing instead. Even then I had a hard time focusing on my music. I loved working in TV news, but I had a hard time writing for deadlines.

I felt like I was always disappointing everyone. I

was terribly discouraged. I wanted to make people proud of me, but I kept coming up short.

You might think I would have been relieved when I was finally diagnosed with ADD . . . but I really wasn't. I felt unfairly singled out. Why would I be given the drive and desire to achieve my dreams, but then be held back by something as frustrating as attention deficit disorder? It wasn't until I turned to the Bible that I was able to make peace with myself and my struggle.

In the New Testament, Paul, one of the early leaders of the church, talked about the "thorn in my flesh" (2 Corinthians 12:7). We don't know what that problem was, but there was some part of Paul's life that frustrated him greatly. I realized that my attention deficit disorder was like a thorn in my flesh. Paul prayed over and over again for his "thorn" to be removed, but God never removed it. Paul discovered that sometimes God allows something difficult to remain in our lives because it makes us stronger and forces us to depend on him more.

So now, as I live daily with my ADD, I know that God will give me the strength I need. And as I seek him, he won't necessarily take away my "thorn," but he will help me learn to live with it—and live to learn from it. And for that, I can honestly say I am blessed.

■ BETHANY SIMPSON

What is the thorn in your flesh? Write down what frustrates you the most about dealing with this problem.

What blessings have you received because of your weaknesses and struggles? What are some ways that you can get daily strength from God to endure this hardship?

How great is the love the Father has lavished on us, that we should be called children of God! And that is what we are!

1 JOHN 3:1

Significance

Lawrence Willoughby was a great employee and well respected at his office. Like many men, he found his significance in his job.

Lawrence's wife, Mandy, was a wonderful mom of their three children, and the neighborhood kids always wanted to be at the Willoughby house. Mandy found her significance in her role as mother.

But at the end of one summer, Lawrence's company was forced to downsize, and he was let go after 28 years of service. The youngest of the Willoughbys began his freshman year at a college 300 miles from home. Lawrence and Mandy were home, alone, with no job, no children, and no sense of significance.

Being wrapped up in our jobs and families might make us better employees and parents, but it might not make us whole people. Finding our significance in the temporary can leave us desperate when things change and times get tough—that's when we find ourselves searching for a greater purpose that will take us through the trials.

Lawrence and Mandy Willoughby had gotten all their significance in life from work and children. When the job and children were gone, so were their purposes for living.

There is a real danger in misplaced significance.

If our self-esteem comes from our jobs and our children and the praise of people, and we lose the jobs and our children move away and the people start criticizing instead—well, you do the math. Depression can sink in because we have a huge empty cavern where our purpose used to be. Purpose, esteem, and significance are very important—so important that we should seek them from the true source.

Many years ago when my job had been going really well, I went from self-satisfaction to depression almost overnight. After receiving accolades for being good at what I do for a living, I lost my ability to work. The experience taught me that I had found my significance in my job. Now that my job was almost gone, so was my purpose for living. Wow, was I shocked.

It was three years before I could work full-time again, but in the process I found my true significance. I can't adequately explain my personal journey, but through prayer and paying attention to God's voice, I accepted that God loves me whether or not I do well in my job, or whether or not my children are at home, at college, or married with children of their own. His love for me is not based on what I do. I am his idea, his creation, his child, and that is a great place to find my significance.

Greg Allen

Where do you get your significance? What makes you feel that life is worth living? Are these things truly worthwhile in the eyes of God and in light of eternity?

God loves you no matter what job you do, or how much money you make, or how great your kids are. How does that fact influence your sense of purpose and worth?

Those who wait on the LORD will find new strength. They will fly high on wings like eagles. They will run and not grow weary. They will walk and not faint.

ISAIAH 40:31, *NLT*

Lazarus Doesn't Live Here Anymore

God has a habit of being late.

For instance, he promised Abraham he would give him a son. Isaac was born 25 years later. King Saul was told by the prophet Samuel to wait seven days until Samuel got back and could perform a sacrificial ceremony for Saul's army. Seven days went by and Samuel was late. So King Saul decided to do the ceremony himself. As soon as the king finished, Samuel showed up, and never mind his tardiness, Samuel was not happy. He told Saul that if he had waited just a few minutes longer, God would have given him a kingdom that would last forever. As it was, Saul lost everything because he had refused to wait on the prophet of God.

Saul learned the hard way. Mary and Martha learned their lesson too. Jesus was late and the consequences were serious. Mary and Martha had sent word to him that their brother Lazarus was sick. They knew that Jesus had healed strangers instantly—opened blind eyes, restored withered limbs. But Lazarus was a friend. Surely Jesus would drop everything and rush to help him. Instead Jesus purposely delayed for two days.

When Jesus finally arrived in the small town of Bethany, Lazarus had been dead for four days.

Martha spoke to Jesus first upon his arrival. "Lord," she said, "if you had been here, my brother would not have died" (John 11:21). When Mary met Jesus she said exactly the same thing. There is such a thing as being fashionably late, and then there is a blatant disregard for the rules of decorum. God, it seems, showed a tendency toward the latter.

God's timing is not our timing. We live inside time, restricted by its boundaries. God has no boundaries. And God's timing is not my timing.

When Jesus reached Mary and Martha, Lazarus had been dead four days. When Jesus said, "Take away the stone," their first thought was that the body would stink (John 11:39). Jesus knew better. He prayed and out walked Lazarus, wrapped head to toe in grave clothes. Everyone was so shocked that nobody lifted a finger to help him get unraveled. Jesus had to tell the crowd to take off the grave clothes (John 11:44). The guy needed to breathe! And in gratitude and wonder, Mary and Martha realized the truth—the truth we all need to understand. God's timing may not be our timing, but one thing you can be sure of: he's never late—he'll arrive just in time.

■ ERIC SNYDER AND PAUL S. WILLIAMS

Does God's timing frustrate you? Why do we find it so hard to wait on the Lord?

Is there something you've been praying about that still has not been answered? If God's timing is perfect, what might be the reason for the delay? Write a prayer asking God for patience to wait on him.

We rejoice in the hope of the glory of God. Not only so, but we also rejoice in our sufferings, because we know that suffering produces perseverance; perseverance, character; and character, hope.

ROMANS 5:2-4

Peace on the Other Side of Pain

With the birth of Jesus came the promise of peace.

When Jesus began his ministry, he called a diverse and unlikely group of 12 to help him carry out his mission. Each man had a different notion of what would be required. Perhaps they had heard of the words of the angel, announcing the arrival of peace on earth. If so they were probably surprised when

Jesus said to them, "Do not suppose that I have come to bring peace to the earth" (Matthew 10:34).

Many assume that peace is achieved by avoiding conflict. However, genuine peace is experienced in deep, intimate community, and deep community seldom emerges until a long, hard winter of discontent has passed.

A famous line written by Graham Greene says, "In Italy, during years of warfare, terror, murder, and bloodshed, the Italians still managed to produce Michelangelo, Leonardo da Vinci, and the Renaissance. In Switzerland, on the other hand, they had five hundred years of conflict-free democracy, and what did they produce? The cuckoo clock."

Pain and conflict are often the birthplace for profound growth. As the old saying goes, "We don't change when we see the light. We change when we feel the heat." It is natural to want to avoid pain and conflict, but we often miss the truth that true peace, like brilliant inspiration, almost always arrives on the heels of chaos.

Unfortunately, most of us avoid conflict and chaos with great purposefulness. As a result, most human relationships are lived in the banal world of pseudo-community. Everyone is nice to everyone else. While such relationships may be great for inventing cuckoo clocks, they are hardly the breeding ground for inspiration, deep community, or genuine peace.

Pseudo-community gives way to mind-numbing emptiness. Many retreat from the pain—the chaos is too troubling, the emptiness too depressing. But for those who forge ahead, committed to growth and relationship, the dark nights of chaos and

emptiness eventually give way to the faint glow
of dawn.

The deepest relationship I know has been
with my wife. As I recount the twists and turns
we've encountered, I wouldn't say it's been a nice
journey. It has often been difficult. But with the full
light of morning, true peace arrives on the wings of
inspiration, born of a deep and honest love.

The followers of Jesus wanted peace on earth.
What they came to understand was that real peace
comes only on the far side of pain. But once they
had tasted of that peace, flowing like cool clear
waters, they understood—it was worth the struggle.

■ PAUL S. WILLIAMS

"Pain and conflict are often the birthplace for profound growth." Take some time to reflect on this quote and write about how it applies to you. How do you deal with pain in your own life—as a learning experience or as unfair punishment?

What trials have served to build character and perseverance in your Christian walk? What specific blessings have come to you on the other side of pain?

Your beauty should not come from outward adornment. . . .
Instead, it should be that of your inner self, the unfading beauty
of a gentle and quiet spirit, which is of great worth in God's sight.

1 Peter 3:3, 4

Beauty Magazines

I don't know about you, but the most dangerous part of the grocery store for me isn't the food. It's the magazine rack.

I can feel perfectly good about myself until I see the toothpick-thin models on the covers of the magazines. Now I know the photos are touched up. I know that many of the women have had plastic surgery, or they work out with personal trainers every day. But still, every time I look at a fashion magazine cover, I gain 15 pounds and my clothes go out of style—just like that. It's enough to make you eat a quart of ice cream in a single sitting.

I recently heard Myrna Blythe in a television interview. Ms. Blythe was the editor of *Ladies' Home Journal* for 20 years. She said, "These magazines peddle the message that women are too fat and too wrinkled, prone to disease, and overworked by our jobs and families."

Too fat and too wrinkled. Wow! Did you get that? These magazines are trying to make us feel fat and ugly. That way we'll buy the magazine to find out how we can become thin and beautiful!

And have you noticed that the definition of beauty has changed? In 1917 the physically "perfect" woman was 5' 4" tall and weighed 137 pounds.

Things have certainly changed! And how about this? Twenty-five years ago, models weighed only 8 percent less than the average woman. Now models weigh 23 percent less than the average woman.

What are the average women to do? Hide in our bedrooms? Hardly. No, what we need is to change the source of our information.

Through Scripture God tells us to focus on that which is true, noble, right, and pure. On things that are lovely and admirable.

And here is the good news: God made *me* lovely. He made *you* lovely. He wants to teach us to live as attractive, admirable people.

God wants to pour loveliness over us—to bathe us in truth and purity. He thinks we're stunning!

When I read in a magazine that my hair's too frizzy
and my shoes are seriously outdated, I feel dimin-
ished. But when I read that God made me lovely
and he thinks I'm beautiful, I feel wonderful. I
guess it's up to me. Who will define my life—a
magazine editor, or the creator of the universe?

BETHANY SIMPSON

What frustrates you about society's emphasis on physical perfection? How do you feel when you compare yourself to that standard of perfection?

Why is it sometimes easier to believe a magazine editor versus our creator and Father when it comes to our appearance? What does it mean to you to think that God sees you as a beautiful object of his love?

If you . . . know how to give good gifts to your children, how much more will your Father in heaven give the Holy Spirit to those who ask him!

LUKE 11:13

Bingo with the Lutherans

When I was 5, after years of saving every penny they could, my parents took our family to Europe.

My brother and I were thrilled. We're part Norwegian and Swedish, and we were able to stay with family in Scandinavia. We ran through the hills around their house chasing baby goats and lambs. We went fishing in the fjord and pulled in nets of flounder. Mom and Dad even bought me a pair of real clogs in a cobblestone market in Copenhagen. I wore them every chance I had.

I believe God loves to bless his children. I always have. And I experienced God's blessings one night on that trip in a way I never could have imagined. It happened in a little Norwegian church where my family played bingo with the Lutherans.

Our family friends took us to the potluck dinner at their little Lutheran church. After dinner they set up for bingo. Bingo was a major cultural event in the Norwegian town of Matre. The prizes included beautiful, hand-painted cutting boards, blankets, food, and lots of other fun things. The prizes looked great to my brother and me. Our dad took special notice of one prize: "I sure don't want to win that ugly green thing, whatever it is." He pointed at a big moss-colored pile of fabric on the stage. It was some kind of furry green blanket.

Armed with several bingo cards and visions of Scandinavian gifts in my travel bags, I set out to enjoy the evening's festivities. The numbers were called out in Norwegian, so we had to listen carefully, and translate into English.

I was amazed when I won the first game. My prize: a hand-painted cutting board. My mom won next. A little later my brother won. We couldn't believe it!

The highlight of the evening, though, was shortly before the games were over. My father finally won. He went up to claim his prize and walked back with a funny look on his face. In his arms was the huge fuzzy green blanket.

Our family trip to Norway was over 20 years ago, but I still curl up with that big green blanket. Inside its folds and wrinkles are the memories of a marvelous childhood. I still have the hand-painted cutting board too. It is one of my prized possessions.

Life is full of little treasures of love, if we open our eyes to see. From fuzzy blankets to cutting boards, to childhood trips to the place of your ancestors, God is at work in the greater scheme of things. He is always reminding us that his love is at work in the world in a thousand tiny ways—even at a bingo game in a little Lutheran church in Norway.

■ BETHANY SIMPSON

As you look back on your life, what are some of
the small, meaningful blessings God has given you?
Take a moment to write them down and thank God
for each of these expressions of his love.

How has God shown his love for you this week?
Make a list of all the little things that bring you joy,
and thank God for his love for you.

He who fears the LORD has a secure fortress,
and for his children it will be a refuge.

PROVERBS 14:26

Storms and Family

A huge storm with straight-line winds blew through my hometown, taking out half the city's power. Approximately 500,000 people were left in the dark in the blink of an eye. The storm lasted no longer than 20 minutes, but its effects lasted days.

As I drove home from my office during the second night of the power outage, I couldn't help but feel alone. It was dark—really dark. No lights in stores.

No street lights to brighten my path—not even traffic lights.

As I pulled into my driveway, I saw little flickers of candlelight through the window, and the loneliness I felt on the drive home evaporated. I heard the sound of my family say, "Hey, Dad." I couldn't see them very well, but I enjoyed the beautiful feeling of hugs from the ones I love the most. While the darkness stayed, the loneliness was gone. I was with family.

About a month before our storm, tornadoes ripped through the little town of Marengo, Indiana. While our storm left us without power, these tornadoes left Marengo without homes, stores, and loved ones. Television news showed helicopter views of Marengo. Trees and telephone poles were scattered like toothpicks. Houses looked like smashed toys.

But when the news switched to a ground camera, I saw a thing of beauty. I saw one family, a family devastated by the loss of everything they had, except for what they were holding on to—each other. They were crying, but smiling too. They were grieving the loss of their home, but they were celebrating the fact that they hadn't lost one another. When the television reporter asked about their situation, they replied, "We've lost everything except each other, but for now that's all we need."

Ben hasn't lost his home to a tornado or even gone without electricity for any length of time. But he has seen worse storms than those in Marengo, Indiana, or in my hometown. Ben lost his job because of a power-hungry boss and has seen his children ridiculed at their school because they don't have fashionable clothes. His wife has even been the source of a few neighborhood jokes because she practices old-fashioned values.

Even so, Ben is one of the most joyful men I know. His little family barely makes ends meet, but they make it work. And the family meets at the dinner table most every night and shares a humble meal, complete with hearty laughs and abundant love. It seems the storms at the office, at school, and in the neighborhood don't affect Ben's family much. As a matter of fact, I'm not so sure they think they've even been through a storm. Secure in the love of God, they have each other. And that's all they need.

■■ Greg Allen

What storms have you and your family been through?
How did you weather them?

When others observe your family during difficult times,
do they see your trust in God? What steps can you take
to strengthen your family's dependence on God so that
it is evident in your everyday living?

When others are happy, be happy with them. If they are sad,
share their sorrow. Live in harmony with each other.

ROMANS 12:15, 16, *NLT*

Firsts

Firsts mark us. They make an indelible impression
on our lives. Most of us remember our first day
of school, our first kiss, and our first day away
at college.

I vividly recall my mom forcing me to wear a bright
orange pleated dress, complete with Peter Pan
collar and bow tie, for the first day of kindergarten.
Mom was ga-ga over my schoolgirl dress, but I was

so unhappy about looking like a pumpkin, I frowned for the traditional first-day-of-school picture.

Over the years my mom has commented about the schoolgirl dress she loved and one of my unforget-table firsts. We laugh that our differences in style started so early.

Recently, my youngest daughter was wiggling her first loose tooth. I jokingly told her to stop because I wasn't ready for my baby to start losing teeth. As you can guess, that only spurred on her efforts.

We were having pizza at a local pizza parlor when Cammy said, "My tooth feels really wiggly now." Her older sisters dragged her off to the restroom so they could assist in their little sister's first tooth loss. A few minutes later, my oldest daughter ran back to the table proclaiming dental victory and handed her dad the bloody tooth.

Cammy was eager to go to bed that night. It was clear she had one thing on her mind—the tooth fairy. She was so excited that she put herself to bed before 7:00. By 8:00 she was asleep, and her older sisters were more than thrilled to play tooth fairies. My 9-year-old offered some dollar bills while my oldest daughter was in hot pursuit of "fairy dust"— otherwise known as glitter.

This first was a really big deal for all of us, not just for Cammy. The older girls and I had a blast playing tooth fairy and Cammy was delighted beyond measure to receive money and glittery evidence of the tooth fairy's visit. I'm quite sure we'll all remember this little event for years to come.

Sharing firsts together—the first time a boy calls, the first time someone rides her bike without training wheels, the first time someone gets his feelings hurt by a friend—bonds us together.

We're told in Scripture, "When others are happy, be happy with them. If they are sad, share their sorrow" (Romans 12:15, *NLT*). That kind of authentic, unconditional love develops over time. Maybe that's why we tend to experience the highs and lows of memorable firsts within the context of family. There should be no safer place to completely blow it or to shine like a star than when surrounded by those who love us no matter what.

 LISA JONES

What are some childhood firsts you remember?
How did your family mark these occasions?

Is your family a safe place to experience life together?
What are some new traditions you could start that
would foster closeness and create lifelong memories
for your family?

Glorious and majestic are God's deeds,

    and his righteousness endures forever.

He has caused his wonders to be remembered;

    the LORD is gracious and compassionate.

PSALM 111:3, 4

Love in Stained Yellow Pine

My wife, Cathryn, is a public school teacher and a tactile learner. She touches everything. She wants to feel the texture of the wooden hull of an old ship. She gently handles the stem of an orchid and brushes the petals against her face. When our children were small, Cathryn would sit and touch the palms of their hands and their tiny fingers for hours at a time.

I am more visually oriented. I don't need to touch, but I must see. Sometimes seeing in my mind's eye is enough, but mostly I want to set my eyes in strong focus on the things that touch my heart.

When she was in junior high, my daughter Jana made a coatrack for me. She was proud but a little self-conscious when she presented her gift to me at dinner on that winter evening. She was afraid I wouldn't like it. Jana knew its flaws.

But to me, of course, the coatrack had no flaws.

Whenever Cathryn visits the office, she rubs her fingers along the curved spine of the coatrack and holds the pegs with her hands.

Every morning when I put my coat on the bottom peg, I study that coatrack like a fine piece of art and behold love in stained yellow pine.

The things Cathryn and I hold dear are not really objects. They are pieces of relationships. Love we can view, study, feel, touch the smooth edges of, and hold close.

But these things are our treasures—Cathryn's and my precious memories embedded with love.

Cathryn and I were in a Cistercian monastery outside Vienna not long ago. The monastery claims to have a piece of the cross on which Jesus was crucified. They received it as a gift nearly a thousand years ago. The piece of wood is encased in gold behind a glass barrier. When Jesus was on the cross, there was no glass barrier. The cross wasn't encased in gold. It was stained with blood. It was rugged.

My wife wanted to touch the cross, but of course, there were velvet ropes and railings and glass. If

Cathryn and I had a piece of that cross, we wouldn't put it in a gold box. We'd keep it right where we could see and touch it, next to every other reminder of the love that has come flooding into our lives.

The kingdom of God is a kingdom of relationships. But for the visually inclined, it doesn't hurt to have a few things to gaze upon lovingly. And for the tactilely inclined, it doesn't hurt to have a few things to touch. And through over 30 years together, the two of us have definitely seen and touched a lot of love.

PAUL S. WILLIAMS

What are your treasures—the things you have kept
because of the love that they remind you of?
What do you remember when you see and touch them?

If you could touch the actual cross where Jesus died,
how do you think touching it would make you feel?
What precious things do you have that remind you of
Jesus' love when you see and touch them?

Taste and see that the LORD is good.

Oh, the joys of those who trust in him!

PSALM 34:8, *NLT*

Stars and Stripes and Smiling Eyes

Uncle Lowell was a man of few words, but he had his own way of telling you that all was well. He did it with his smiling eyes.

Outside of those expressive eyes of his, you didn't get much of an indication of how he felt about anything. Ever. But I could always count on those smiling eyes.

With the honeysuckle in bloom and the side yard filled with clover, tiny green grapes wrapped in giant leaves hanging from the arbor, and the smell of fresh cut hay coming from the barn, I could always count on smiling eyes from Uncle Lowell on the Fourth of July. I don't know how many July Fourth holidays were spent with Aunt Lela and Uncle Lowell in Grayson, Kentucky, but they are the only Independence Days I remember from my childhood.

Midway through the heat and humidity of the afternoon, charcoal was lit and meat was placed on the grill. Aunt Lela and Mom would send us to get the watermelon from the cool cellar. Potato salad, baked beans, and iced tea were brought to the old picnic table under the oak tree. Hamburgers and hot dogs were eaten, and the adults all talked about how this year's July Fourth parade down Main Street was the best ever.

Meal completed, I dug into the watermelon, spit seeds into the clover, and watched Uncle Lowell's eyes smile.

The parade was always fun. The meal was always scrumptious. Playing with my cousins occupied the better part of the day. But the highlight of my holiday was when Uncle Lowell put together the ice cream churn and started cranking. Cream and sugar and other mysterious ingredients were put into the center of the contraption. Ice was packed around it. Then Uncle Lowell, eyes smiling their brightest, turned that crank until everything was just right.

Aunt Lela called us over and gave each of us a bowl of homemade ice cream. With the fireflies blinking and the charcoal embers dying, we settled onto our blankets, turned our eyes to the southeast sky, and watched fireworks.

In my adult years, I've seen the finest fireworks that money can buy burst over the New York skyline, but I've never seen anything finer than the Grayson, Kentucky, fireworks on the Fourth of July.

Every July Fourth, when I see flags flying in the breeze and backyard barbecues fired up all over the neighborhood, I think of homemade ice cream, bursting fireworks, and smiling eyes.

Life is an accumulation of ordinary memories. But when strung together and seen in the light of grace, if you look carefully, you can see the smiling eyes of God.

■■ PAUL S. WILLIAMS

What are your most fond memories of the simple blessings you've received throughout your life? Whose smiling eyes, kind words, or warm hospitality bring a smile to your face when you remember them?

What ordinary, everyday things show you the grace and love that your heavenly Father has for you? List all the little blessings you can think of and thank God for each of them today.

Suddenly, a great company of the heavenly host appeared with
the angel, praising God and saying,
"Glory to God in the highest,
> *and on earth peace to men on whom his favor rests."*

LUKE 2:13, 14

Time-Honored Traditions

Every Christmas Eve my wife and I sit in front
of the Christmas tree with our children and read
stories.

We've been reading the same stories since the chil-
dren were small. The books are very old and every
illustration is marvelously detailed. One book with
a green cover etched in gold contains my favorite
Christmas picture—St. Nicholas peering into the

bedroom of two young boys in what appears to be an old English cottage. The boys are fast asleep, dreaming of sugarplums.

When I was a child, I was one of those boys. My dreams were of bicycles and train sets and Grandma's homemade biscuits on Christmas morning. Though my children are now grown, we still read from these old richly textured Christmas books handed down through the generations.

Before I read those stories to my children, my parents read them to me and their parents to them. There is comfort and strength and wisdom in those stories and in the telling of them.

The last story we read every Christmas Eve is Luke's biblical account of the birth of the Christ child. The children sit quietly with the dog at their feet, the lights flickering on the evergreen. With

every Christmas, we hold our breath at the drama
of this ancient story—the fate of the entire world
resting on a child born in a barn.

The mystery of this tale is too much to compre-
hend. As our family of five hears those sacred
words, our thoughts go far away to a place we can-
not fully understand where a father sacrifices his
Son for the sake of a world that has lost its way.

And in those quiet moments of warm and lovely
silence, we five are united, secure in the know-
ing that this one story holds us all together with a
thread that cannot be broken.

Our family ends our Christmas Eve drama with a
short prayer, a walk outside to look at the stars, and
a good tucking into bed for all. At least once each
year, every single human being should be tucked
into bed. It's good for the soul.

And into the sweet night we go, with our family traditions in our hearts, visions of Christmas morning in our heads, and the beautiful security of knowing that God is with us and we are where we always have been—nestled securely in his heart.

PAUL S. WILLIAMS

What are your favorite Christmas traditions?
What makes them special to you?

What touches you the most about the Christmas story?
How can your Christmas traditions celebrate the gift of
Christ in meaningful ways?

Every good and perfect gift is from above, coming down from the Father of the heavenly lights, who does not change like shifting shadows.

James 1:17

A Wonderful Blessing

I had never heard of him before and had no idea he existed. But after taking my daughters to school one spring morning in 1998, I picked up a bagel and an iced tea from the store, along with my morning copy of the *New York Times*. There was nothing out of the ordinary in the paper that day. But something in the obituaries caught my eye. Dr. Louis Saunders had passed away in Dallas, Texas. Dr. Saunders was the minister who presided at the graveside service of Lee Harvey Oswald in 1963. That obituary was memorable. I cut it out and set it aside on my desk. I wasn't sure why, but I just had a sense I might need it later.

Not quite a year after that, I was writing scripts for a Worship Television Network shoot in New Hampshire. I picked up the article, reread it, and began writing. Once the script was completed, I kept on writing until I had completed an expanded story that became part of my first book, *Laughter, Tears, and In-Between*.

We shot the script in the White Mountains of New Hampshire, and it began airing shortly thereafter. A few months after the show began airing, the Worship Network received a letter from Bette Blair, a friend of the widow of Dr. Saunders. Bette wrote to say that Mrs. Saunders was suffering from cancer, and she asked if the network could locate a copy of the tape and forward it to the Saunders family since they had not yet seen the program.

We immediately sent the tape and a copy of my book to the Saunders family. Mrs. Saunders wrote me soon thereafter.

Her letter was written in her own hand, and she apologized for the quality of her penmanship. She wrote, "I have cancer, you know, and it's painful to do very much, including pick up a pen and paper."

Her letter was three pages long, and she wrote very kindly of the honor I had given her husband in telling his story. She told me a little about her three children and asked me to pray for her family. Her kind and gracious letter let me know that she and her husband had been cut from the same cloth. It was abundantly clear that they were salt-of-the-earth kind of people.

Mrs. Jeanne Saunders passed away not long after I received her letter. Her friend sent me a copy of the funeral program and eulogy. She had been deeply loved by many people. I was just glad to have brought a little bit of recognition to her husband and a moment of joy to her final days of suffering.

Every now and then God touches our lives in ways we never imagined, and we are blessed beyond measure. These touches are gifts—gifts that give us pause from the daily routine and remind us of the glorious mystery at work in the world, reconciling the creation to the creator.

■■ PAUL S. WILLIAMS

How has God touched your life in unexpected ways?
What seemingly little things has he done that later
turned out to be life-changing for you or someone else?

What specific gifts has God given you recently?
How might you use those gifts to pass on God's love
to others?

Blessed are those who have learned to acclaim you,
who walk in the light of your presence, O LORD.

PSALM 89:15

Pictures

A picture paints a thousand words—at least that is
what we have been told.

Recently, I was looking at some photos of our fam-
ily vacations. At the time the pictures were taken,
our boys were in grade school and our daughter
was just a toddler. Now our two oldest kids are in
college, and that baby girl is in middle school. Our
lives are changing.

Already we have seen the difference in our home. We no longer have five schedules to juggle, and our house has grown a little quieter. It's easier to get a table for three at most restaurants. Since our daughter doesn't drive yet, there's no waiting up for a car to pull in, no arguments over curfew—at least not yet. I am enjoying the change and feeling sad about it all at the same time.

As I look at my family photos, I find the thing I focus on the most is me. I keep wondering what I was thinking when those pictures were taken. Did I realize how quickly time would pass? Did I anticipate both the laughter and tears my kids would bring?

Frankly, some pictures look like I was thinking about the next project I had to complete or the work on my desk. I wish I could step back into those pictures and relive some of them. Knowing what I know now, I would have enjoyed the moments more when our family of five was all together as one.

But of course, we can't step into the picture and live the days over again. We knew what we knew then and no more. Life is played out one moment at a time.

I felt obligated recently to tell my sons to enjoy their time in college. "These days will go quickly," I promised. The look in their eyes told me they didn't believe me any more than I believed my Dad when he told me the same thing. "But look at the pictures," I wanted to say.

Don't misunderstand. I'm not sitting in a rocker wishing for my life back. In fact, in many ways I'm enjoying the emptier nest my wife and I now share. Our daughter certainly thinks having her brothers out of the house isn't all bad.

Our family still takes a lot of pictures. Only now I am more aware of what I am thinking when each picture is taken. Am I enjoying this moment with my family? Am I grateful to God for the blessings he has poured out onto our lives?

I do wish the younger version of me had been more attentive to the things that really matter—laughter and family and love. As for future years, when I look back on the pictures we're taking now, I wonder what new wisdom and insight I will have gained. I wonder what I'll know then that I wish I knew now.

Life is a continuing journey, and the more we learn to love those closest to us, the less we'll have to regret later. So put on your best smile and take some pictures—save some memories.

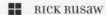   RICK RUSAW

What do you see when you look at pictures from your past? What do you wish you could go back and change?

What do you hope you will see when you look back on pictures you're taking now? How can you cherish your loved ones now so that you'll have no regrets later?

Enter his gates with thanksgiving
and his courts with praise;
give thanks to him and praise his name.
For the LORD is good and his love endures forever.

PSALM 100:4, 5

The Brevity of It All

I think that what I like most about Thanksgiving is the brevity of it. Christmas is one long marketing season these days. And with New Year's just one week later, the season seems to drag on forever.

Easter is great, but the date is confusing. You never know when it's coming. I still don't understand how they calculate its arrival. I think somebody just throws darts at a calendar of spring Sundays. When

Easter does finally come though, it usually means a weeklong vacation from school, especially if it coincides with Passover.

Thanksgiving is different. Unlike Christmas and Easter, Thanksgiving is just one day of celebrating. That's it. No more. So whatever it is you're going to do, you'd better get started, because in 24 hours, it's history.

Now that my children are older, I love Thanksgiving more than ever. The holiday begins on Wednesday evening, with everyone arriving home from college with lots of stories to tell. Conversation lingers well into the night, and sleep comes with peace, knowing we are all again under one roof.

Thanksgiving morning starts late for everyone except Mom. She's in the kitchen early, doing mysterious things with wonderful smelling foods. A morning run is usually in order for me. Then I rake the leaves one final time before the snows of winter. When he hears the rustle of the raked leaves, my son Jonathan stumbles out of bed to help. Sometimes the girls jump in. When they were little, they literally jumped in—into the big piles of leaves left by our sugar maple and two giant oaks.

With appetites awakened, we all head inside to the delicious smells and warm anticipation of the Thanksgiving meal.

In our house Thanksgiving dinner always includes turkey, stuffing, sweet potatoes, corn and lima casserole, green beans, salad, and homemade bread. Pumpkin and cherry pies complete our family feast. After the feast we push back our chairs and talk. We speak of dreams and hopes and memories, of trips to the hills, and roads not taken, and all the marvelous "what ifs" that remain.

All this happens in just one day—a single marvelous day of Thanksgiving, where all good things are harvested in their time, and the life of one little family is celebrated from its roots to its God-blessed fruit.

Yes, I think Thanksgiving is my favorite holiday of all.

■■ PAUL S. WILLIAMS

What are your family's Thanksgiving traditions? What are some of your best memories of Thanksgivings past?

What do you have to be thankful for today? As the song says, "Count your blessings—name them one by one." Take some time to write a list of all the wonderful blessings God has given you—and don't forget to thank him for them all.

The righteous will flourish like a palm tree. . . .
They will still bear fruit in old age,
     they will stay fresh and green.

PSALM 92:12, 14

Alma

With the overconfidence born of a fresh college diploma, I was truly as green as green could be. On a bright summer day I began my life of ministry with a visit to a shut-in, 85-year-old Alma. I assumed I'd find an elderly and lonely lady living in a dark and dingy apartment decorated with pictures of yesteryear.

Boy, was I wrong.

I knocked, Alma opened the door, and there stood a tiny bundle of energy and joy. "Thanks for coming, Greg! Come in, come in," she said. As Alma led me to her dining room table to talk, I recognized the smell filling the room—homemade chocolate chip cookies. They were delicious. My preconceived notion of sitting in a dark apartment creating boring conversation with a little elderly lady was so wrong. Alma's laughter, jokes, and stories brought sunshine to the place. My college degree paled in comparison to the diploma of experience and wisdom earned by Alma.

As I walked out the door to go to my office (and mail back my diploma!), Alma said, "Oh, Greg, wait a minute, I almost forgot." She handed me another dozen of those wonderful cookies wrapped in green plastic wrap. "Thank you so much for spending time with me today," she said. What an education. I learned that shut-in didn't mean what I thought.

Eighty-five-year-old Alma taught me that, even if a person can't drive or even walk very far, it doesn't mean that person doesn't have a life.

As a result of those summer days spent chatting with Alma, I learned the value of simply listening. We didn't have a think-tank meeting or an in-depth prayer session. We just chatted—about her husband, now gone to be with the Lord, or about my future wife. She often repeated her favorite stories. When I returned to the office, if someone asked me if I'd visited a shut-in I took offense. With a mouthful of chocolate chip cookies, I'd answer, "If you mean, was I with Alma, that wise saint, then, yes, that's where I was."

When I'm unable to drive or get out of the house and somebody calls me a shut-in, I pray that I'll have half the wisdom of Alma. I hope I'll greet the young person who visits me with warm chocolate chip cookies and old stories of joy and hope and love. I'll tell them what Jesus taught. He said we are to love God and to love people. And I'll tell them about Alma, who loved me. And when the gentle soul who visits me turns 85, I hope he'll tell the same stories to yet another young visitor, as the chain of love that is the gospel of Christ continues unbroken.

■ Greg Allen

Have you ever visited a shut-in or a hospital patient,
expecting a sad, depressed person, and instead found
that person full of joy? How did that experience affect
you? How did you feel when you left?

What do you think brings such joy to people in not-
so-joyful circumstances? What are some ways you can
serve and encourage them (and in turn learn about the
joy in their lives)?

I have learned the secret of being content in any and every situation, whether well fed or hungry, whether living in plenty or in want. I can do everything through [Christ] who gives me strength.

PHILIPPIANS 4:12, 13

Island of Tranquility

In 1704, Alexander Selkirk took a huge risk. He was the sailing master on a British warship that had arrived on the remote island of Juan Fernandez, 400 miles off the coast of Chile. The ship had faced several battles and severe weather, and was in serious need of repair.

The captain wanted to continue sailing. Selkirk, however, was so certain of the ship's impending doom that he asked to be left on the uninhabited island. The captain granted his request. Selkirk took with him a few provisions, some tools, and a Bible. The British warship departed, leaving Alexander Selkirk to wait.

Selkirk assumed it wouldn't take long for another ship to pass by the island and rescue him. But weeks of waiting turned into months. He became so depressed and lonely that he considered suicide. But then a transformation occurred.

The island actually had a very nice climate. There was plenty of fresh water and fruit. Spanish ships had left goats on the island, which supplied Selkirk with endless meat and milk. A population of cats prevented rodents from eating his food supply. Selkirk found a convenient cave in which to settle and began a daily ritual of exercise and spiritual devotions. What began as loneliness and poverty became what he later called a "tranquility of solitude." And when he was rescued four years and four months later, his experience also became the basis for the first great English novel.

> After several years on a deserted island a stranded sailor wrote, "I learned to . . . consider what I enjoyed, rather than what I wanted. I thought of those discontented people who cannot enjoy comfortably what God has given them, because they see and covet something that He has not given them. All our discontents about what we want appeared to me to spring from the want of thankfulness for what we already have."

These words, however, are not those of Alexander Selkirk, but of the character that his true story inspired—Daniel Defoe's *Robinson Crusoe*. After hearing the story of Alexander Selkirk, Defoe

This is what the Sovereign LORD, the Holy One of Israel, says:
"In repentance and rest is your salvation,
in quietness and trust is your strength."

ISAIAH 30:15

The Treadmill of Life

You've probably seen one of those television comedies in which the star of the show is running on a treadmill. The person is jogging along when the treadmill picks up speed and the runner flashes a no-problem-I-can-handle-this smile. But in a matter of seconds, the runner's smile fades as he dramatically falls off the speeding treadmill, defeated by the exercise equipment.

Now that's pretty funny on a TV sitcom, but in real life it's dangerous. You can be badly hurt falling off a moving treadmill.

It's equally serious when you act as if your entire life is one swiftly moving treadmill that's picking up speed, and you don't know how to slow it down. The best you can hope to do is keep your legs moving—fast. How do we keep our balance when life has us running at a breakneck pace?

Unfortunately, balance is a virtue I have not yet mastered. I pay serious attention to the Scriptures that say I should be busy at home and not be lazy, but I pay far less attention to the passages that invite me to a life of peace and rest. What's the key to achieving a godly balance?

One afternoon as I was busy tackling the never-ending mountain of laundry that our household creates, I found some dirty clothes bunched up in my 4-year-old's dresser. Exasperated, I yelled, "How many times have I told you to put your dirty clothes in the hamper?" Impatience, exhaustion, irritability—all signs that my treadmill's moving way too fast.

It's amazing how the face of a child can bring a message from God. I had yelled at my daughter— inappropriately. The hurt on her face brought me to my senses. My life was running out of control, and I had a problem. I was the problem.

As I sorted the clean clothes from the dirty ones, I began to cry. I thought, *What's wrong with me?* I'd always been able to handle a lot of pressure. I could multitask with the best of them. But the tears still flowed. My body was sending me a signal, and God was speaking. "Slow down, stop trying to do it all. Who are you trying to impress?"

I finally slowed down long enough to learn the lesson God had been trying to teach me: genuine peace and contentment are not determined by the pace of your treadmill. True joy is found by getting off the treadmill and onto the path that allows you to seek God's plan for your life. You can follow that path at a reasonable pace because God is walking with you. He helps you move faster when you need to, and he slows you down at the first sign of weariness. He helps align your ambitions according to his good purpose. And, unlike a treadmill, walking a path actually gets you somewhere!

As I watch my children playing on carefree, sun-drenched days, or napping peacefully as the rain patters on the window, I hear the whisper of God: "Slow down. This life is meant to be enjoyed. Remember, walk the path with me. Get off the treadmill."

 LISA JONES

Are you on a treadmill getting nowhere or on a path, traveling with God at his pace? What are some ways that you could increase the balance in your life?

Who are you trying to impress? Is it necessary? How might you go about impressing your heavenly Father?

Ruby n. Durden

Ruby

Durden